Facts About the Rock Dove

By Lisa Strattin

© 2016 Lisa Strattin

Revised 2022 © Lisa Strattin

FREE BOOK

FREE FOR ALL SUBSCRIBERS

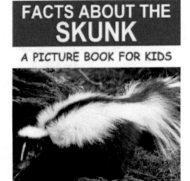

LisaStrattin.com/Subscribe-Here

BOX SET

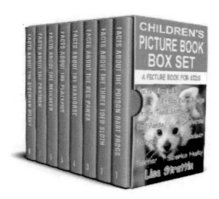

- **FACTS ABOUT THE POISON DART FROGS**
- **FACTS ABOUT THE THREE TOED SLOTH**
- **FACTS ABOUT THE RED PANDA**
- **FACTS ABOUT THE SEAHORSE**
- **FACTS ABOUT THE PLATYPUS**
- **FACTS ABOUT THE REINDEER**
- **FACTS ABOUT THE PANTHER**
- **FACTS ABOUT THE SIBERIAN HUSKY**

LisaStrattin.com/BookBundle

Facts for Kids Picture Books by Lisa Strattin

Little Blue Penguin, Vol 92

Chipmunk, Vol 5

Frilled Lizard, Vol 39

Blue and Gold Macaw, Vol 13

Poison Dart Frogs, Vol 50

Blue Tarantula, Vol 115

African Elephants, Vol 8

Amur Leopard, Vol 89

Sabre Tooth Tiger, Vol 167

Baboon, Vol 174

Sign Up for New Release Emails Here

LisaStrattin.com/subscribe-here

COVER IMAGE

https://www.flickr.com/photos/92384235@N02/39910151880/

ADDITIONAL IMAGES

https://www.flickr.com/photos/taylar/27725574101/

https://www.flickr.com/photos/joegoauk73/29120423561/

https://www.flickr.com/photos/i8ipod/16661776874/

https://www.flickr.com/photos/infomastern/27880490641/

https://www.flickr.com/photos/infomastern/28142608560/

https://www.flickr.com/photos/128325945@N05/42501251160/

https://www.flickr.com/photos/pamas/15804974198/

https://www.flickr.com/photos/infomastern/10119476706/

https://www.flickr.com/photos/128325945@N05/43591778294/

https://www.flickr.com/photos/126816719@N03/16710121638/

Contents

INTRODUCTION

The Rock Dove is commonly known as a *Rock Pigeon*.

Wild Rock Doves have a colorful head and are pale grey with two black bars on each wing.

It has a dark bluish-gray head, neck, and chest with a glossy yellowish, greenish, and reddish-purple color along its neck and wing feathers.

The iris of its' eye is orange, red or golden with a paler inner ring. The bare skin around the eye is bluish-grey. The bill is grey-black, and feet are purplish-red.

The males and females look almost identical. The white lower back of the pure Rock Dove is its most distinctive feature; the two black bars on its pale grey wings are also a differentiator from other doves. The tail has a black band on the end. The outer web of the tail feathers are margined with white.

It is strong and quick when flying, dashing out from sea caves, flying low over the water, its lighter grey rump showing well from above.

Young birds show little luster in their coloring. The eye color of the bird is generally orange, but a few may have white-grey eyes. The eyelids are orange and are surrounded in a grey-white eye ring. The feet are red to pink.

When circling overhead, the white underwing of the bird becomes visible. Although it is a relatively strong flier, it also glides through the air a lot of the time. It goes to fields of grain and green food occasionally, but it is not considered much of a pest to farmers.

When disturbed, a Rock Dove in a group will take off in flight with a noisy clapping sound.

HABITAT

The Rock Doves live in various open and semi-open environments. Rock ledges and cliffs are used for nesting and breeding in the wild. They have been found wild in Europe, North Africa, and western Asia.

At the present time, they have established themselves in cities all around the world. The species is abundant, with an estimated population of around 17 to 28 million wild birds!

Rock Doves have adapted to "human encroachment" on their natural habitat very well. They nest on skyscrapers, bridges, old farm buildings and even under our decks.

SIZE

The adult Rock Dove is 11 to 15 inches long with a
24 to 28 inch wingspan.

Average weight for wild Rock Doves ranges from 8-
13 ounces, but overfed domestic and semi-domestic
birds can get very fat.

DIET

Rock Doves feed on the ground alone or in flocks. They roost together in buildings or on walls or statues. When drinking, most birds take small sips and tilt their heads backwards to swallow the water. But the Rock Doves are able to dip their bills into the water and drink continuously without having to tilt their heads back.

HABITAT

The Rock Dove has a natural range in western and southern Europe, North Africa and into South Asia. They are often found in pairs during the breeding season. The Rock Dove originated in southern Asia and their existence dates for centuries.

Its preferred habitat is the natural cliffs, usually on coasts of water. But it does very well in cities with many people as well.

LIFE SPAN AND LIFE CYCLE

A Rock Dove lives for 3-5 years in the wild, but in captivity it lives for around 15 years.

This dove mostly breeds in peak times of spring and summer. In India, they breed in February. They make nesting sites along coastal cliff faces, as well as the artificial cliff faces created by apartment buildings with nearby racks or roof spaces.

Their nest is made of straw and sticks, laid on a ledge, under cover, often on the window racks of buildings. Two white eggs are laid at one time. The pair of male and female birds share the incubation period of 17 to 19 days. The newly hatched dove has pale yellow down and a flesh-colored bill with a dark band. The mother feeds the baby for the first few days on pigeon's milk. It is able to leave the nest when it is about 30 days old.

FRIENDS AND ENEMIES

Almost all predatory birds are enemies of the Rock Doves. They are prey for several raptor species who live in urban areas. Falcons and Eurasian Sparrow Hawks are natural predators of pigeons. Some of the other common enemies of Rock Doves are opossums, raccoons, Red-Tailed Hawks, gulls, crows, ravens, and Eastern Screech Owls.

On the ground, the adults, their young and their eggs are at risk from domestic cats. Humans beings have always fed pigeons and they are good friends of the Rock Dove.

SUITABILITY AS PETS

Rock Doves are one of the oldest domesticated birds. Common city pigeons are actually European Rock Doves. They are understood to be the same bird as the one that Noah released from the ark, which returned with the olive branch to signify the end of the Great Flood. Nearly all religions revere pigeons as holy birds.

They are good for the environment, as they eat food we dispose of as litter. Anyone who has one of these birds as a pet will attest to their loyalty and affection. They make excellent friends.

Often, pigeons are the only form of life in an otherwise bleak urban landscape. Feeding pigeons is well recognized by the medical community as a good means of relaxation and interacting with them provides people with relief from stress.

COLOR ME

COLOR ME

COLOR ME

COLOR ME

COLOR ME

COLOR ME

COLOR ME

COLOR ME

COLOR ME

COLOR ME

Please leave me a review here:

LisaStrattin.com/Review-Vol-36

For more Kindle Downloads Visit Lisa Strattin
Author Page on Amazon Author Central

amazon.com/author/lisastrattin

To see upcoming titles, visit my website at
LisaStrattin.com– most books available on
Kindle!

LisaStrattin.com

FREE BOOK

FOR ALL SUBSCRIBERS – SIGN UP NOW

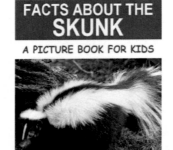

LisaStrattin.com/Subscribe-Here

LisaStrattin.com/Facebook

LisaStrattin.com/Youtube

Made in the USA
Coppell, TX
23 August 2022

81909399R00026